NBAMEGASTARS

By Bruce Weber

SCHOLASTIC INC.
New York Toronto London Auckland Sydney

Photo Credits
Cover(Kemp), 15, 21: NBA/Andy Hayt. **Cover(Robinson)**: NBA/Noren Trotman. **5, 18, 22(inset), 23**: NBA/Andrew D. Bernstein.
4, 14: NBA/Richard Lewis. **Back Cover(Olajuwon), 6, 7, 25**: NBA/Nathaniel S. Butler. **Cover(Hardaway), 9, 11, 22**: NBA/Barry Gossage.
10, 26: NBA/Sam Forencich. **12, 13, 24**: NBA/Scott Cunningham. **16, 30**: NBA/Layne Murdoch. **17**: NBA/Allen Einstein. **19**: NBA/Lou
Capozzola. **Cover(Olajuwon), 27**: NBA/Bill Baptist. **28**: NBA/Fernando Medina. **31**: NBA/Chris Covatta. **Back Cover(boy)**: Gary Gold.

ISBN 0-590-13769-7

© 1997 by NBA Properties, Inc.
All rights reserved. Published by Scholastic Inc.

12 11 10 9 8 7 6 5 4 3 2 1   7 8 9/9 0 1 2/0

Printed in the U.S.A.
First Scholastic printing, February 1997
Book design: **Oberlander Design**

Who's Tom Fox?

Just one of the busiest NBA officials in the world.

Fox's job?

He runs the league's marketing operation in Asia!

The Chinese, among others, are just bananas over pro basketball, *American* style.

Look out, world. Here comes Hoops!

American pro basketball is rapidly becoming the **world's** game. Anybody who has ever tossed a round ball toward a 10-foot high basket watches the NBA megastars in **awe**...

The **power** of Shaq,

the ballet **beauty** of Michael,

the **grace** of Grant,

the incredible **toughness** of the Mailman.

That's what makes NBA basketball the game *the world wants to watch*.

So when the best teams representing the nations of the world came to Atlanta last summer, they knew they were in for an uphill battle against America's Dream Team.

But the visitors weren't unhappy.

They were delighted just to be on the same court with **Hakeem** and **Penny** and the rest of the NBA's best.

And, not by chance, the world also wants to wear anything with an **NBA** logo on it— which keeps Tom Fox busy in Hong Kong all year-round.

Charles Barkley

TRADED TO THE
HOUSTON ROCKETS
· AUGUST 1996 ·

Whenever a college superstar comes to the NBA,

he is often compared to current and past pros.

"He's the next Magic [or Kareem or Michael]," they'll announce.

But nobody has ever been trumpeted as "the next Barkley."

That's because some wise person threw away the mold.

There's only one Barkley and that's good news.

Sir Charles

Barkley continues to fool those who were willing to write him off years ago. "Too short and too wide for a power forward," they said. But the man can shoot, rebound, dish, play defense, and lead his team like nobody's business. "Sir Charles," as he has been known since his college days (Auburn), is one of only ten NBA players ever to surpass 20,000 points and 10,000 rebounds. Not bad for a 6'4 1/2" (actual height) player battling opponents five inches or more taller.

It's the mouth, however, that places Barkley in a class by himself. The big guy has an opinion on absolutely everything and is never afraid to express it.

- Two-time Olympic gold medalist: 1992, 1996
- Ten-time NBA All-Star
- League MVP for 1992-93
- MVP of the 1991 All-Star Game
- First-round draft choice of Philadelphia (fifth player overall) in 1984

"As a fan seeking the ultimate in NBA entertainment, one can only admire Charles Barkley."

—Cherokee Parks

FUN FACT

Charles was cut from the 1984 U.S. Olympic Team by Indiana coach Bob Knight.

CAREER STATS:

POS	G	Min.	FG%	3 Pt.%	FT%	Reb.	Ast.	Stl	Blk	TP	PPG
F	890	32,932	.550	.269	.738	10,311	3,495	1,451	818	20,740	23.3

Patrick Ewing

Patrick Ewing owns New York.
In a city that supports several professional sports teams,
the Knicks rank as one of the fans' favorites.
And Patrick Ewing, now well into his second decade as a Knick,
is the guy who makes New York's team go.

King of New York

CAREER HIGHLIGHTS

- Ten-time NBA All-Star
- New York's all-time leading rebounder and scorer
- Two-time Olympic gold medalist: 1984, 1992
- Number one pick of 1985 NBA draft
- Led Georgetown to 1984 NCAA title

On many nights, he carries the load and leads his team to victory.

At a time in his career when others begin to lose their taste for the NBA grind, Patrick is just as committed as he was on his first day in the Garden. He enjoys victories and takes losses hard. His work ethic is unbelievable. And when he swoops across the lane and goes to the bucket for the finger roll or slam dunk, he's awfully hard to stop. Few players his size have owned his outside range.

When he hangs it up — and that might not be for another three or four years — he'll have a permanent spot in the hearts of New Yorkers.

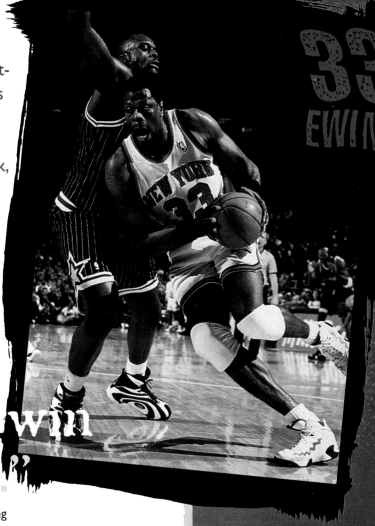

"In New York, when you win it's heaven."

— Patrick Ewing

FUN FACT

Call him Mr. Hollywood. Patrick had cameo roles in three films: The Exorcist 3, Funny About Love, and Space Jam.

CAREER STATS:

POS	G	Min.	FG%	3 Pt.%	FT%	Reb.	Ast.	Stl	Blk	TP	PPG
C	835	30,516	.515	.159	.744	8,679	1,803	910	2,327	19,788	23.7

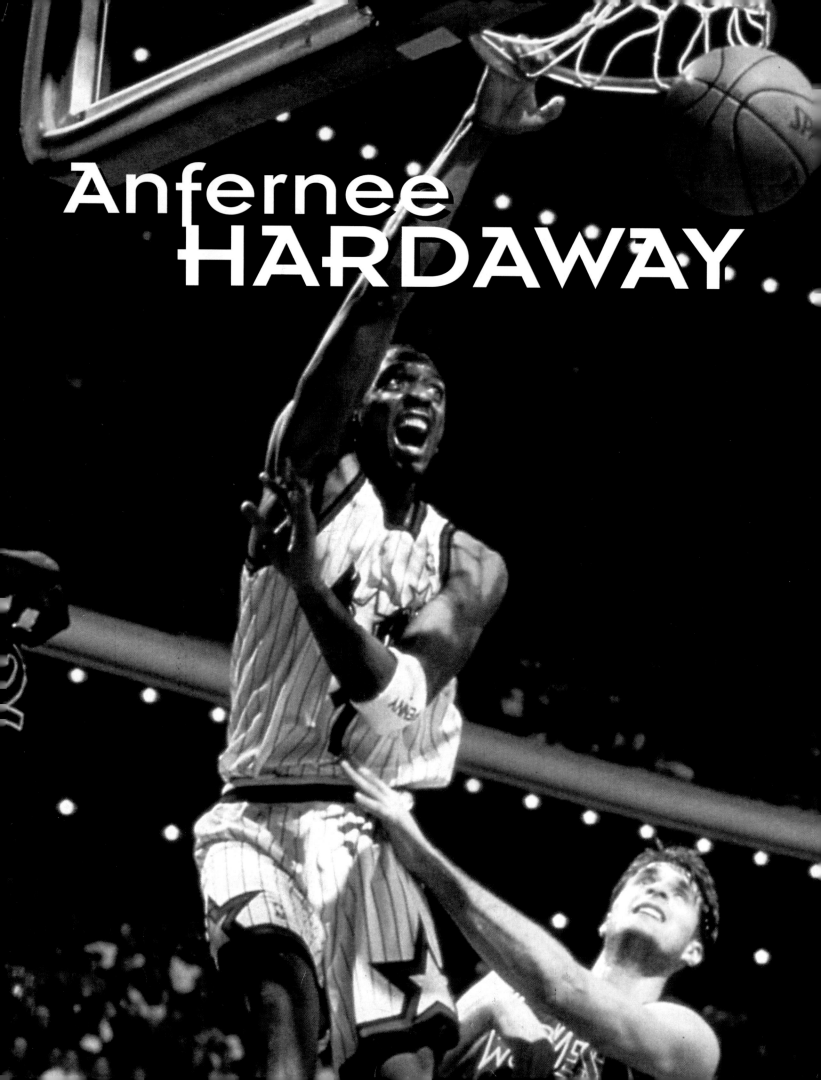

Anfernee
HARDAWAY

- Olympic gold medalist: 1996
- Two-time NBA All-Star
- Led Magic to 1995 Eastern Conference title
- Third overall pick of 1993 draft

Okay, Orlando fans.

Those of you who booed Anfernee Hardaway before his first Magic game in 1993, stand up. C'mon now. You did, didn't you?

When Orlando picked Michigan's Chris Webber in the '93 NBA Draft, Orlando rooters thought they'd have the newest twin towers (Webber and Shaq). Then the Magic dealt Chris to the Warriors for Penny and three future first-round picks. The fans weren't pleased.

THE REAL DEAL

But not for long. Hardaway has become the engine that drives the Magic. He does it all from the point: dishing the rock, hitting the trey, going to the basket for a slam of his own, playing defense like crazy, and more. He (and "teammate" Little Penny) have even become wildly popular in a series of television commercials. Hardaway's the real deal.

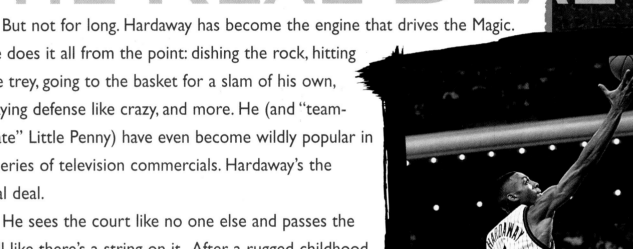

He sees the court like no one else and passes the ball like there's a string on it. After a rugged childhood in Memphis, Penny has it all going his way now. He's one of the league's top point guards and many believe that one day, he'll be its best player.

"HE'S THE FINEST ALL-AROUND GUARD IN THE NBA. IF THERE'S A **BIG PLAY** IN THE GAME, COUNT ON PENNY TO BE INVOLVED."

— Dave Wohl, Miami Heat

FUN FACT

Anfernee got the nickname "Penny" from grandmother Louise Hardaway, who raised him. "He's as pretty as a penny," she announced—and it stuck.

CAREER STATS:

POS	G	Min.	FG%	3 Pt.%	FT%	Reb.	Ast.	Stl	Blk	TP	PPG
G	241	8,931	.498	.314	.762	1,129	1,679	486	118	4,706	19.5

Michael Jordan

It's just about the most identifiable name in the world.

Sure, there's Madonna.

And there once was an artist formerly known as Prince.

But almost anywhere on the globe,

the single name Michael has just one meaning.

Just Michael

Maybe you get restless when your grandfather drones on about having seen Joe DiMaggio

or Ted Williams play baseball

or Jimmy Brown tote a football.

But fifty years from now, you'll be telling your grandkids about a spectacular hoopster named Michael Jordan.

"He could do so many magical things with a basketball," you'll say. That fadeaway jump shot, the hang-in-the-air layup that began at the foul line, that three-point bomb whenever the Bulls really needed it. And, you'll crow, "He might have been even better on defense!"

"He's the best player on our planet. I'd pay money to see him play."

— Indiana Coach Larry Brown

FUN FACT

Born in Brooklyn, N.Y., Jordan moved to North Carolina at age seven. As a ninth-grader he was cut from the junior varsity hoop squad at Laney High School.

CAREER STATS:

POS	G	Min.	FG%	3 Pt.%	FT%	Reb.	Ast.	Stl	Blk	TP	PPG
G	766	29,600	.512	.332	.844	4,879	4,377	2,025	739	24,489	32.0

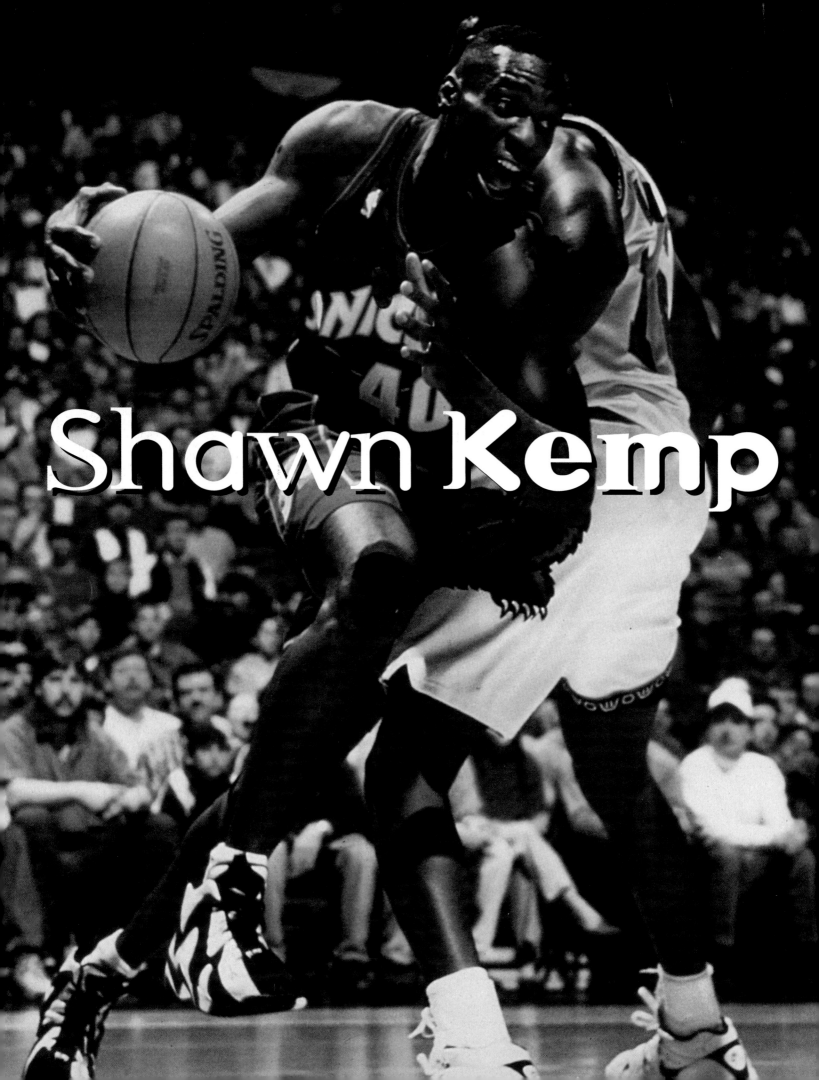

Shawn Kemp

- Four-time NBA All-Star
- Starred for Dream Team II, gold medal winners of the '94 World Championship of Basketball
- Successfully jumped to the NBA without playing college ball

In Seattle, known around the country for its annual heavy rain, Sonics fans are engaged in a little spelling practice. They've changed the name of megastar Shawn Kemp to "Reign Man." Around Washington, he's the king—dominating the airspace between 8 and 12 feet off the floor.

Reign Man

After he failed to qualify academically for college play, Kemp became the first draft pick of Seattle in the 1989 NBA Draft. Sonics fans booed heartily. They don't anymore. "Shawn always responded to a challenge," remembers his high school coach, Jim Hahn of Concord High School in Indiana. "Taunting Shawn was the best way to make him play better."

The 6'10", 240-pounder, a seven-year pro at age 26, outworks everybody—in and out of season. He uses his long, hard-as-rock arms to fullest advantage. In both speed and endurance, he's determined to win an NBA Championship. And if he gets much better, he may have to be declared illegal!

"There aren't many players capable of staying with him. Shawn's intensity is his **weapon** of **greatness**."

—Seattle Coach George Karl

FUN FACT

Shawn and his high school buddies spent considerable time planning their college days. But they never happened for Kemp. Now he's planning to go to college during the offseason, which will delight his mom, Barbara.

CAREER STATS:

POS	G	Min.	FG%	3 Pt.%	FT%	Reb.	Ast.	Stl	Blk	TP	PPG
F	554	15,859	.522	.222	.728	5,171	940	650	878	8,632	15.9

Jason
Kidd

- Played in his first All-Star Game in 1996
- Co-Rookie of the Year (with Grant Hill) in 1995
- Second overall pick of 1994 NBA Draft

Jason Kidd has been a marked man for years. Way back in the eighth grade in the Bay Area, Kidd was already labeled as a star in the making. Forget the "making." He's there now.

Strong & Smooth

Following four years at tiny St. Joseph's of Notre Dame High School near Oakland (they went 122-14 with Jason) and two years at the University of California, Kidd was the prime pick of the Mavericks, who passed on Grant Hill in the draft. Jason made an instant impact, helping the Mavs improve by 23 wins in his rookie year.

Kidd was delighted when his favorite football team, the Raiders, returned to Oakland last season. Maybe the Oakland Raiders of his youth contributed to his basketball playing style—like a linebacker. There may not be a tougher point guard in the world. At 6'4" and 210 pounds, Kidd has all the power he needs to dominate a ball game. More important, however, is his decision making. There isn't a young player anywhere with the court savvy of this Kidd.

"You already hear players saying, 'I wish I played with him.' That's so uncommon for a young player."

—Seattle Coach George Karl

FUN FACT

Kidd set his first scoring record in the fourth grade. He scored 21 of his team's 30 points in a Catholic League game.

CAREER STATS:

POS	G	Min.	FG%	3 Pt.%	FT%	Reb.	Ast.	Stl	Blk	TP	PPG
G	160	5,702	.383	.311	.695	983	1,390	983	50	2,270	14.2

Karl Malone

- Nine-time NBA All-Star
- Seven-time All-NBA First Team pick
- Two-time All-Star Game MVP: 1989, 1993
- Two-time Olympic gold medalist: 1992, 1996
- Passed the 23,000-point mark in 1996

Karl Malone is a workingman's kind of player. There's nothing fancy about him. He doesn't float, hang, or spin. There's no ballet in the Mailman— not at regular speed or even in slow motion. He's a classic banger.

The Mailman

He muscles down a rebound, pitches to the wing, runs down the court, takes a pass, knocks down anything in his way, and powers in for a layup. It's simple, pure basketball, with a lunch-pail approach.

Malone owns the kind of body others envy. He's 6'9" and 256 pounds of pure muscle. Only a sculptor could make a body better than Karl's. When NBA insiders argue about the greatest power forward, it's always Malone vs. Barkley. Fortunately for U.S. Olympic fans, Karl and Charles have played together on two Dream Teams.

Karl always does what's needed to win. Whether it's the 51 points he threw in against Golden State last season, or playing almost every minute when the going gets tough, this Mailman always delivers.

32 MALONE

"If you've watched Malone, you've got to know this guy is a monster player."

—Charles Barkley

FUN FACT

Karl once owned a trucking business. And when the company needed a driver to direct an 18-wheeler between Utah and Louisiana (Karl's birthplace), Malone jumped into the driver's seat.

CAREER STATS:

POS	G	Min.	FG%	3 Pt.%	FT%	Reb.	Ast.	Stl	Blk	TP	PPG
F	898	33,801	.525	.283	.722	9,733	2,815	1,304	756	23,343	26.0

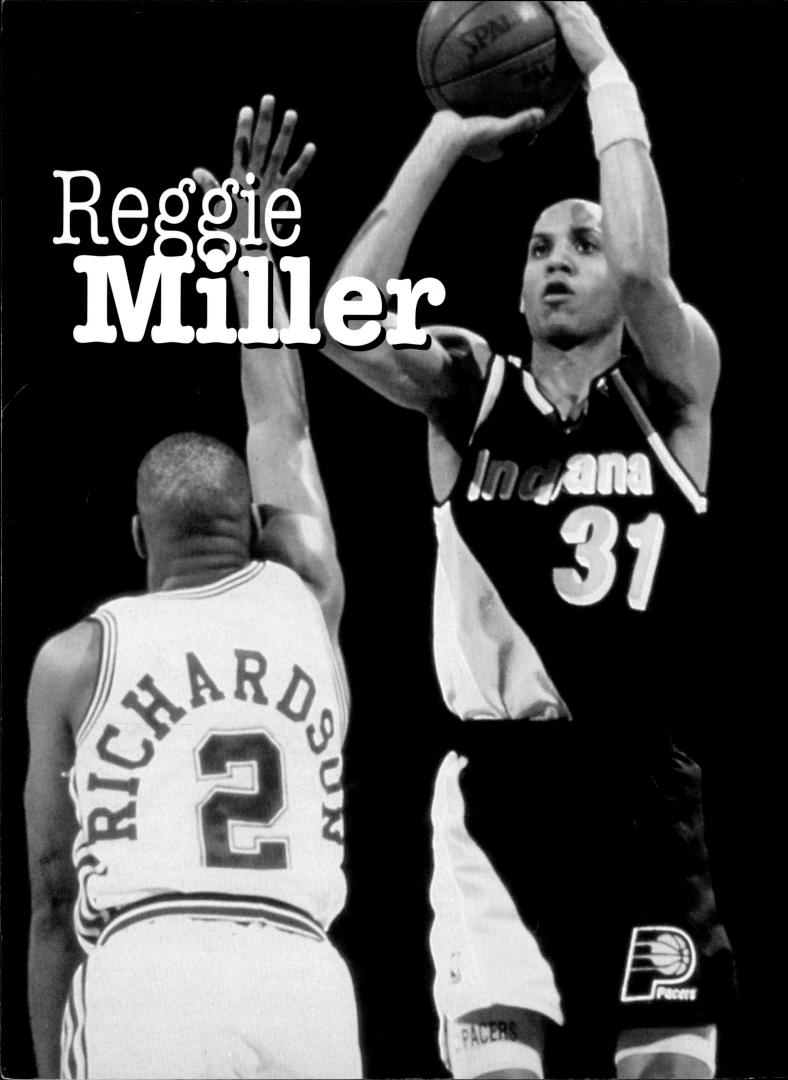

Reggie Miller

They won't forget Reggie Miller in New York anytime soon. Come playoff time, Miller seems to show up at Madison Square Garden ready to rock the hometown Knicks.

The Pure Shooter

CAREER HIGHLIGHTS

- Two-time Dream Teamer: 1994, 1996
- Three-time All-Star
- After only eight seasons, all-time Pacer leader in eight stat categories
- First-round draft pick in 1987

Scoring from practically anywhere on the court, a red-hot Reggie almost single-handedly beat the Knicks in Game 5 of the 1994 Eastern Conference playoffs, then brought the Pacers back from six down with 18 *seconds* to go to win a playoff game in 1995. Movie director Spike Lee, the world's biggest Knicks fan, was blown away—as were the other 19,000 at the Garden.

That's what Reggie Miller does, draining threes from impossible angles and distances. When you think you have Indiana buried, Miller pulls them back up by their sneaker laces. When he's out of the lineup, as he was for most of the '96 playoffs, the Pacers suffer.

Lots of fans see the highly competitive, in-your-face Miller as a classic bad guy. They couldn't be more wrong. He's probably the most community-minded Pacer, working hard for charities like the United Negro College Fund and visiting children's hospitals all over the area.

"He's looked at as one of the **best players** in the league. He deserves that."

— Indiana Coach Larry Brown

FUN FACT

Reggie comes from one of America's most-athletic families: His sister Cheryl is arguably the greatest woman basketball player ever, sister Tammy played volleyball for Fresno State, and brother Darrell was a catcher for the California Angels.

CAREER STATS:

POS	G	Min.	FG%	3 Pt.%	FT%	Reb.	Ast.	Stl	Blk	TP	PPG
G	720	24,538	.491	.397	.877	2,270	2,320	884	184	14,073	19.5

Hakeem Olajuwon

In Houston, Hakeem Olajuwon is known as "The Dream."

Dream On

CAREER HIGHLIGHTS

- Olympic gold medalist: 1996
- Led Rockets to consecutive NBA Championships: 1994, 1995
- Named NBA MVP, Defensive Player of the Year, and Playoff MVP: 1994
- Paced University of Houston to three straight NCAA Final Fours

But to any defender trying to stop him, Hakeem becomes a living nightmare.

Toughness, like beauty, seems to be in the eye of the beholder. Michael Jordan may be the best all-around outside player, but inside, Hakeem is in a class by himself. He just seems to invent moves designed to get him to the basket. No one seems to be able to out-rebound him.

Born in Lagos, Nigeria, Hakeem came to basketball late. At age 15, he was playing team handball (it's a little like soccer, but you can use your hands). His high school team was playing in a tournament when he got a chance to try basketball. It worked instantly, and Hakeem quickly became a national team player in his new sport. The rest, as they say, is history.

Hakeem played on the U. S. Olympic Basketball Team in 1996 after becoming an American citizen in 1993. He continues to visit his Nigerian homeland frequently.

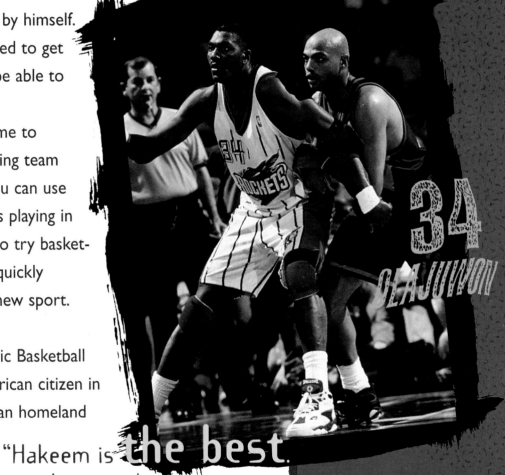

34 OLAJUWON

"Hakeem is the best. He can score from the outside. Inside. Spin. Dip underneath. Steal the ball. Block shots.

He's like a seven-foot guard."

—Michael Jordan

FUN FACT

Originally came to America to attend St. John's University in New York City. But it was so cold when he got there, he jumped on the next plane to Houston, where he has been (University of Houston, Houston Rockets) ever since.

CAREER STATS:

POS	G	Min.	FG%	3 Pt.%	FT%	Reb.	Ast.	Stl	Blk	TP	PPG
C	900	33,981	.516	.184	.711	11,023	2,392	1,694	3,190	21,840	24.3

Shaquille O'Neal

SIGNED WITH THE
LOS ANGELES LAKERS

• JULY 1996 •

- Four-time All-Star
- 1993 NBA Rookie of the Year
- NBA scoring leader: 1995 (29.3 points per game)
- Two-time Dream Teamer: 1994, 1996

Is there a more fearsome sight than Shaquille O'Neal lifting off for one of his patented throw-it-down dunks?

Probably not.

The Shaq Attack

At 7'1" and 300-plus pounds, Shaquille Rashaun O'Neal owns one of the largest bodies in the universe. And when he powers off the floor on his way to the hole, the best advice for his opponents is simply, "Get out of the way."

Shaq also owns one of the best-known smiles anywhere. But his joy certainly doesn't spread to NBA rivals. Now a star for the Los Angeles Lakers, Shaq continues the Laker tradition of great centers. First there was Wilt Chamberlain, then Kareem Abdul-Jabbar, and now Shaquille O'Neal. But the most important Laker tradition is winning NBA Championships. With mighty Shaq inside—posting up strong, ripping down rebounds, and blocking shots—the Lakers can stake their claim as title contenders for years to come. That remains Shaq's greatest challenge: Can he help the Lakers regain the championship glory of years past?

"The rest of the league is scared. Got to be."

— Dennis Scott

FUN FACT

An all-around star, Shaq has cut two rap albums (Shaq Diesel and Shaq Fu: da Return) and starred in two movies (Blue Chips and Kazaam).

CAREER STATS:

POS	G	Min.	FG%	3 Pt.%	FT%	Reb.	Ast.	Stl	Blk	TP	PPG
C	295	11,164	.581	.091	.546	3,691	716	243	824	8,019	27.2

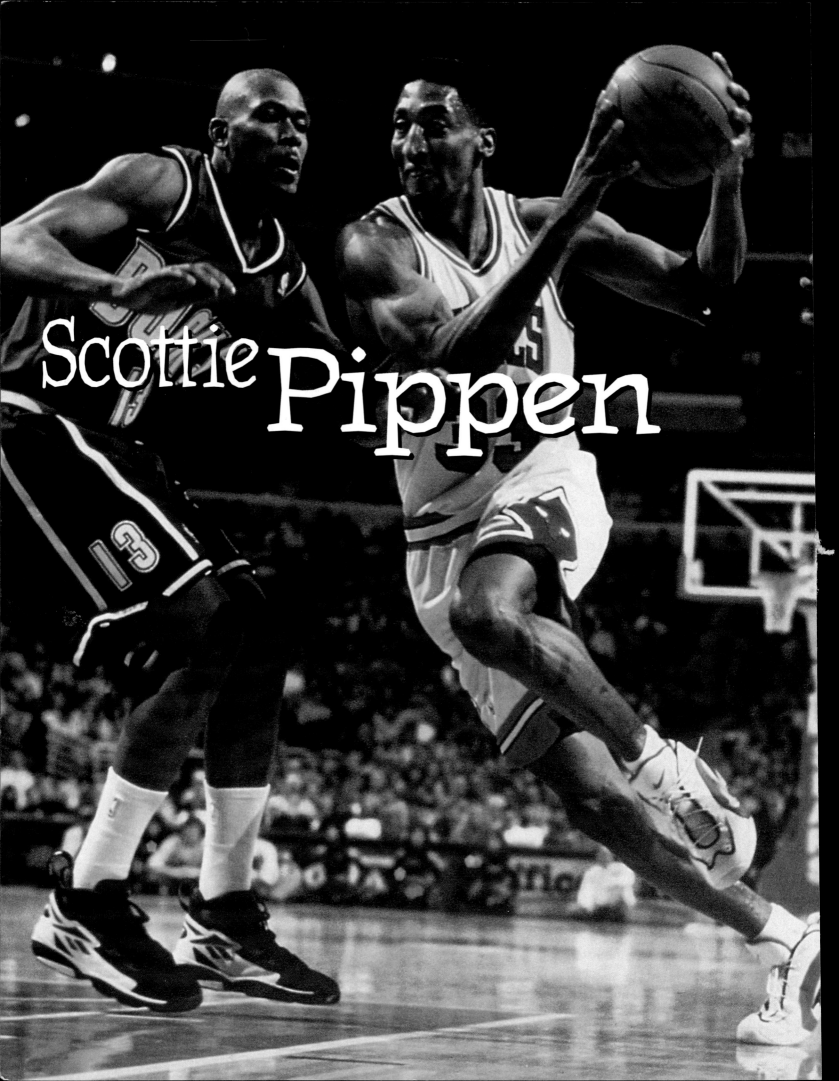

Scottie Pippen

- Six-time NBA All-Star
- Two-time Olympic gold medalist: 1992, 1996
- Five-time member of All-Defensive team
- Helped lead Bulls to four NBA titles: 1991, 1992, 1993, 1996

Virtually anywhere else in the NBA, Scottie Pippen would be the main man. In Chicago, of course, there's Michael — which means that Pippen takes a backseat. But experts know that without Scottie, that handful of NBA Championship rings might have found their way to cities other than Chicago.

All-Around Winner

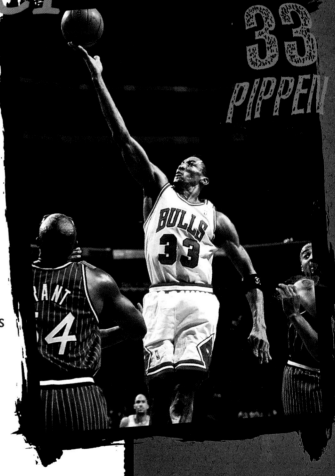

The Bulls are fortunate to have the 6'7", 225-pound Pippen because of his versatility. Back in college (Central Arkansas), Scottie was forced to play virtually every position, learning skills that would help him excel as a pro. He has the passing ability of a point guard, rebounds like a power forward, scores like a shooting guard, and plays defense as well as anyone in the NBA.

The youngest of twelve children, Scottie wasn't much of a high school player. He actually began his college career as a student manager, getting a chance to play only when several players were injured. By his senior year, he averaged 23.6 points and 10 rebounds per game. NBA scouts quickly realized that Scottie had lots of potential.

The Bulls were especially lucky to have him when Jordan temporarily retired in '93. Pippen stepped into the leadership role, scoring more than 22 points per game.

"The *excitement of* winning a championship is overwhelming."

—Scottie Pippen

FUN FACT

Scottie began his NBA career, if only momentarily, with the Seattle SuperSonics. The Sonics picked Pippen in the first round of the 1987 NBA Draft—but then traded his rights to the Bulls.

CAREER STATS:

POS	G	Min.	FG%	3 Pt.%	FT%	Reb.	Ast.	Stl	Blk	TP	PPG
F	707	25,110	.486	.317	.687	4,900	3,723	1,538	677	12,490	17.7

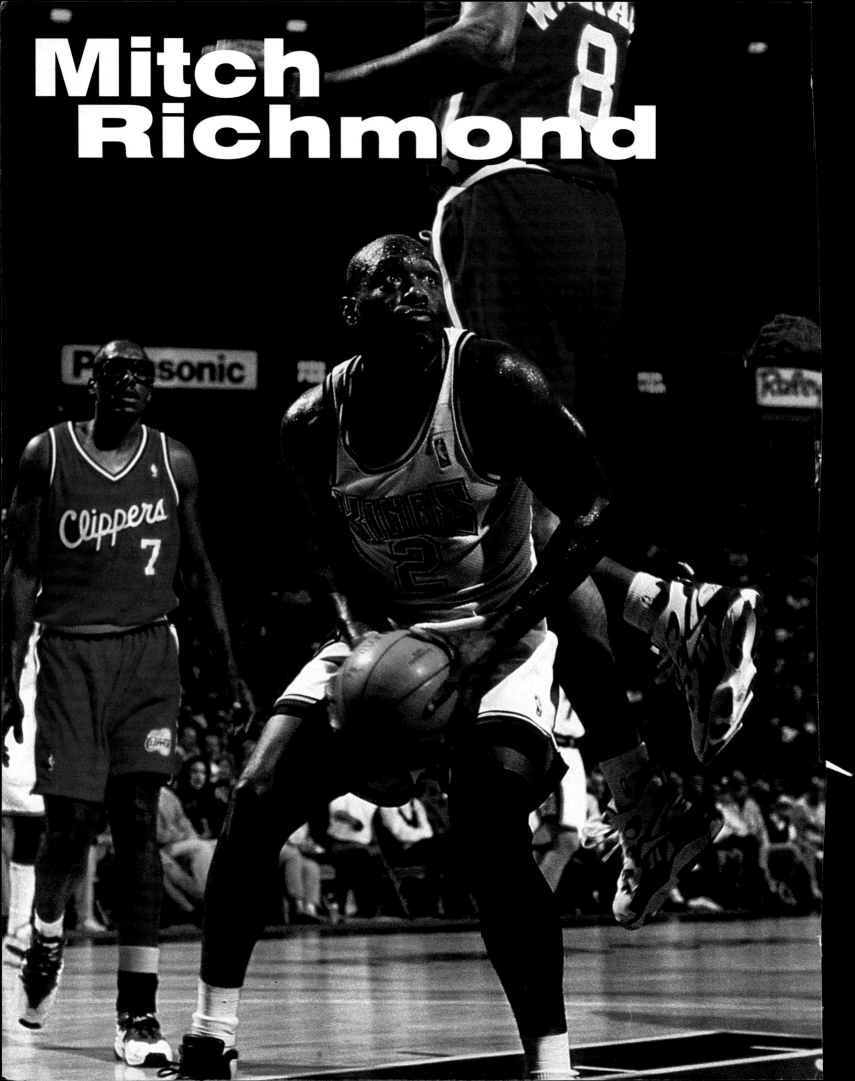
Mitch
Richmond

Ever since coming to the Golden State Warriors back in 1988, Mitch Richmond has been only one thing: consistent.
He scores consistently (22.8 points per game, seventh among active players), passes consistently, plays defense consistently,

- Four-time NBA All-Star
- MVP of the 1995 All-Star Game (10–13 from the field, 3–3 three-pointers)
- Rookie of the Year: 1989
- Olympic gold medalist: 1996

and gives an all-out effort every night.

Built to Score

What he is *not* is flashy, trash-talking, or selfish. Bottom line: The ex-Kansas State star is someone a coach loves to have on his team.

The ultra-competitive Richmond finds ways to beat you every time down the floor. He'll post up, shoot from the perimeter, or drive past his man. Double up on him and he'll find the open man. Cover him one-on-one and he'll put the ball in the hole.

At a sturdy 6'5", 215 pounds, Mitch is built like an NFL tight end. That enables him to overwhelm some of the NBA's smaller guards. But when he can't do that, he's perfectly capable of stepping back and hitting for three — all night long.

RICHMOND

"I'll tell you what he's all about. He's about **winning**."

—Sacramento Coach Garry St. Jean

FUN FACT

Mitch breaks up his teammates by performing dead-on imitations of virtually every star in the NBA.

CAREER STATS:

POS	G	Min.	FG%	3 Pt.%	FT%	Reb.	Ast.	Stl	Blk	TP	PPG
G	600	22,381	.466	.393	.840	2,665	2,306	2,665	179	13,653	22.8

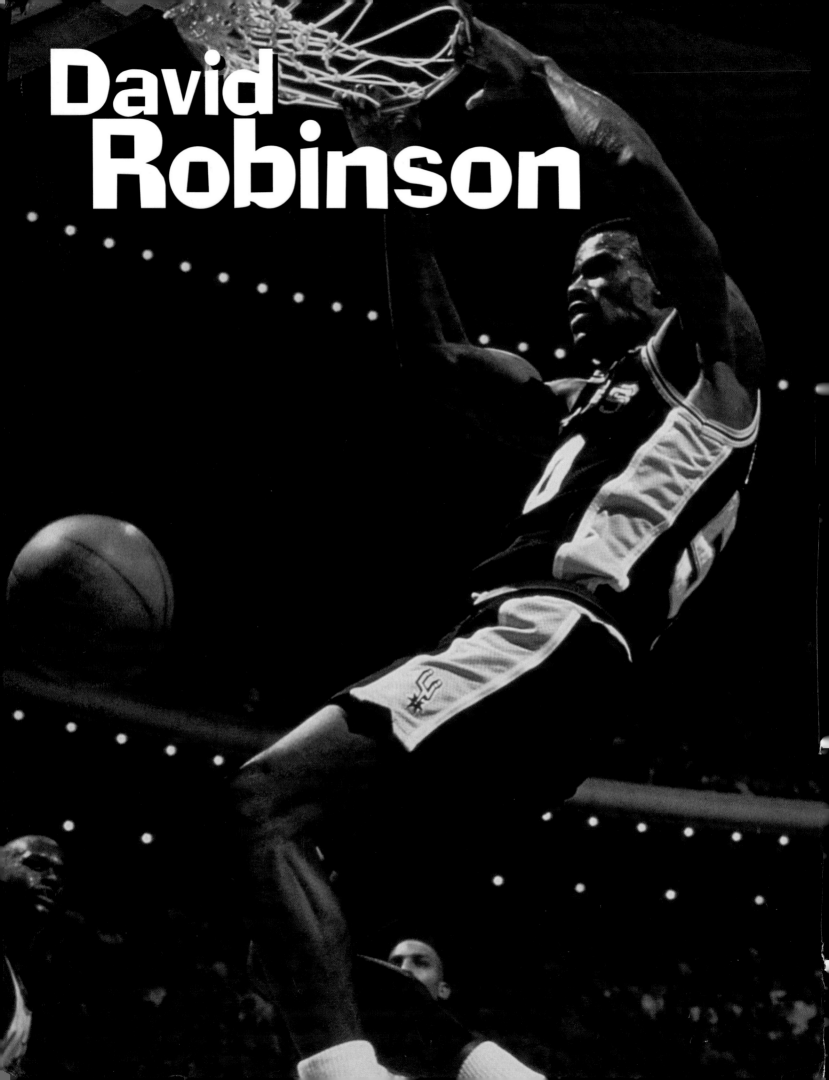

David
Robinson

San Antonio's David Robinson embraces the opportunity to be a role model, and nobody does it better. It's not only the points and rebounds and blocks and hustle. Mr. Robinson excels in everything he does: a 1320 SAT score, a degree in math from the U.S. Naval Academy, outstanding musical ability, leadership on and off the court.

The Admiral

- 1995 NBA Most Valuable Player
- Led league in scoring: 1994 (29.8 ppg)
- Scored a career-high 71 points vs. the Clippers in 1994
- Three-time All-America at the Naval Academy
- Served two years in the U.S. Navy before joining the Spurs
- Three-time U.S. Olympian: 1988, 1992, 1996

Though he has only been in the league for seven years, Robinson is already the Spurs all-time leader in rebounding and shot-blocking. David has accomplished just about every imaginable personal achievement, but it is a team goal that drives him now. The Admiral won't rest until he takes the Spurs all the way to an NBA Championship.

Still, David realizes he can't do it alone. "I'm a little more relaxed now," says David. "A few years ago, I knew I was expected to carry the team every night. No more. If I have a bad game, we have enough talent to pick us up."

"David is a true role model for all kinds of people of all ages. He is, unquestionably, the most admired citizen in San Antonio."
—former Spurs chairman Robert F. McDermott

50 ROBINSON

FUN FACT

While most NBA players spent their childhood polishing their basketball skills, David Robinson enjoyed building computers.

CAREER STATS:

POS	G	Min.	FG%	3 Pt.%	FT%	Reb.	Ast.	Stl	Blk	TP	PPG
C	557	21,206	.526	.261	.747	6,563	1,718	934	2,006	14,260	25.6

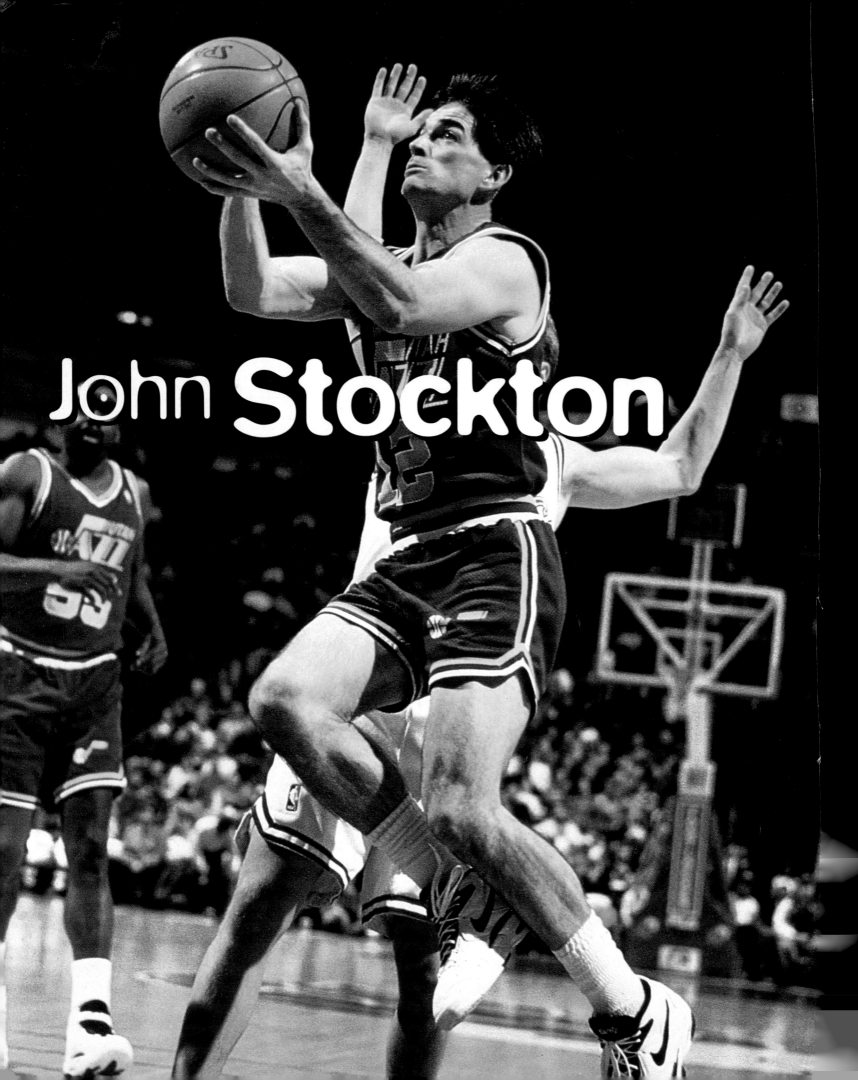

John **Stockton**

If you're thinking about playing point guard,

get a Utah Jazz game tape and study John Stockton.

There simply isn't any better instructional material. The NBA's all-time assist leader, Stockton has amazing court vision, great court sense, and an incredible work ethic.

The Playmaker

If there's a loose ball anywhere, John is willing to sacrifice his body to get it.

Karl Malone has probably been the biggest recipient of Stockton's giving. Both of them have a shot at basketball's Hall of Fame when they retire. "If we're fortunate enough to go," says Malone, "I hope they put both of us in together. We're bonded. I've often been asked what I'd do without him. I don't want to think about it."

Stockton downplays his passing success. Superstars Oscar Robertson and Magic Johnson were among the previous all-time assist leaders. "It's just a statistic," says Stockton. "I just don't put myself in a class with those guys." Current NBA players and coaches are quick to disagree.

"John has fun playing basketball. I think that's his greatest asset, his attitude."

—Utah Jazz president Frank Layden

- Surprising first-round pick of Jazz in 1984 draft
- Two-time Olympic gold medalist: 1992, 1996
- Three-time All-NBA Defensive Team
- All-time NBA steals leader

FUN FACT

John might not have been Gonzaga University's all-time best athlete. His grandfather starred for GU's greatest football team (1924) and was voted All-America at quarterback!

CAREER STATS:

POS	G	Min.	FG%	3 Pt.%	FT%	Reb.	Ast.	Stl	Blk	TP	PPG
G	980	31,930	.517	.378	.821	2,605	11,310	2,365	201	13,285	13.6

ODDS & ENDS

1996 ALL-NBA TEAM

- F Scottie Pippen
- F Karl Malone
- C David Robinson
- G Michael Jordan
- G Anfernee Hardaway

1996 NBA ALL-DEFENSIVE TEAM

- F Scottie Pippen
- F Dennis Rodman
- C David Robinson
- G Gary Payton
- G Michael Jordan

SCHICK 1996 ALL-ROOKIE TEAM

Damon Stoudamire, *Toronto*

Joe Smith, *Golden State*

Antonio McDyess, *Denver*

Jerry Stackhouse, *Philadelphia*

Michael Finley, *Phoenix*

Arvydas Sabonis, *Portland*

1995 - 1996 NBA AWARD WINNERS

NBA Most Valuable Player
Michael Jordan

IBM Coach of the Year
Phil Jackson

Schick Rookie of the Year
Damon Stoudamire

NBA Defensive Player of the Year
Gary Payton

NBA Sixth Man
Toni Kukoc

NBA Most Improved Player
Gheorghe Muresan

BRUCE WEBER'S 1996-97 PLAYOFF PICKS

ATLANTIC DIVISION

1. New York Knicks
2. Orlando Magic
3. Washington Bullets
4. Miami Heat
5. Philadelphia 76ers
6. Boston Celtics
7. New Jersey Nets

CENTRAL DIVISION

1. Chicago Bulls
2. Indiana Pacers
3. Cleveland Cavaliers
4. Milwaukee Bucks
5. Detroit Pistons
6. Atlanta Hawks
7. Charlotte Hornets
8. Toronto Raptors

MIDWEST DIVISION

1. Houston Rockets
2. San Antonio Spurs
3. Utah Jazz
4. Dallas Mavericks
5. Denver Nuggets
6. Minnesota Timberwolves
7. Vancouver Grizzlies

PACIFIC DIVISION

1. Seattle SuperSonics
2. Los Angeles Lakers
3. Sacramento Kings
4. Phoenix Suns
5. Portland Trail Blazers
6. Golden State Warriors
7. Los Angeles Clippers

EASTERN CONFERENCE CHAMPIONS
Chicago Bulls

WESTERN CONFERENCE CHAMPIONS
L.A. Lakers

NBA WORLD CHAMPIONS
Chicago Bulls